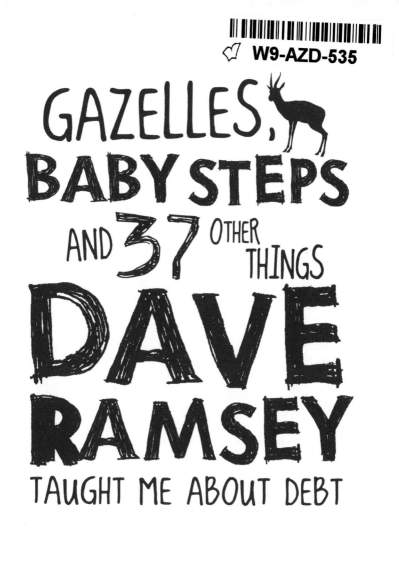

GAZELLES, BABY STEPS AND 37 OTHER THINGS DAVE RAMSEY TAUGHT ME ABOUT DEBT

BY JON ACUFF

© 2010 Lampo Licensing, LLC
Published by Lampo Press, The Lampo Group, Inc.
Brentwood, Tennessee 37027

This publication is designed to provide accurate and authoritative
information with regard to the subject matter covered. It is sold with
the understanding that the publisher is not engaged in rendering
financial, accounting or other professional advice. If financial advice or
other expert assistance is required, the services of a competent
professional should be sought.

Editors: Allen Harris and Darcie Clemen
Cover design: Daniel Bell
Illustrations: Blake Barton, Ben Lalisan, and Melissa McKenney
Interior design: Mary Hooper, Milkglass Creative

ISBN: 978-0-978-56209-0

TABLE OF CONTENTS

CONTENTS

CONTENTS

INTRODUCTION

I went broke 20 years ago. I mean, I went *seriously* broke. Seven-figures broke. As a young real estate investor, I had made a whole lot of stupid decisions, and the weight of that stupidity came crashing down on my young family. We were sued a bazillion times. The sheriff's deputy delivered lawsuit papers to our house so often that we started inviting him in for cookies!

You know what I remember most about that time? I remember how alone we felt. We were so ashamed of what was going on that we hid it from everyone. We didn't think anyone would be able to understand what we were going through or relate to some of the decisions we had made. We didn't think anyone could have been as boneheaded as we were.

We were wrong.

The truth is, as I started working with families going through this exact same situation, I discovered that *everyone* feels alone when they're standing in a financial mess. But when you put a few of these families together and get them talking, they all discover that a lot of the horror stories aren't just *familiar*—they're actually kind of funny.

Other couples fight about money. Other people owe more on their cars than they make in a year. Other people got a foreclosure notice in the mail last week. Those are the ones we'd expect.

But guess what? Other people hate buying bridesmaid dresses. Other people get mad at their friends for inviting them to expensive, exotic destination weddings. Other people think $.99 is too much to pay for a game to play on a phone they spent $400 on in the first place. Other people financed their cat.

You're not alone.

Too often, our money problems grow into some kind of monster hiding in the closet, growing bigger and badder and scarier every day that we keep them hidden. But if we want to change the behaviors that get us into trouble, we've got to kick the monster out of the closet—and laugh at him.

And I don't know anyone better equipped to do this than Jon Acuff. Through his blog and book, *Stuff Christians Like*, Jon's proven that he has a unique perspective on life that helps us get the joke and get the truth behind the joke every time. Lucky for us, Jon decided to chronicle his observations on his own journey toward Financial Peace. Think of it as an insider's guide to the "Dave Ramsey" stuff we all laugh about.

Do your former credit card companies stalk you like a deranged ex-girlfriend? *Page 45.*

Do you need to baby-proof your home against 27-year-old kids trying to move into your basement? *Page 19.*

Have you ever made the basket walk of shame? *Page 173.*

Was your biggest question throughout *Financial Peace University* "How many blue shirts does Dave actually own?" *Page 13.*

This book had me on the floor, laughing, because it's real life. And behind the goofy things we do with money, you'll see the persistence, dedication and do-or-die hard work that is changing lives all over the country. So dig in and get ready for some fun. You've got gazelles, Baby Steps and 37 other things to learn about debt.

—Dave Ramsey

HOBBIES EAT MONEY

If you're a guy, you kind of always wanted to play guitar. I don't care if you grew up in the country or the city, by the beach or in the mountains, in the '60s or the '90s, every guy on the planet knows that guitar players are cool. And I like to be cool, too, so I once got a guitar.

But because hobbies are the hungriest money-eaters ever, I didn't just get a regular old acoustic guitar. We never buy equipment based on our current skill level. We usually buy the equipment we'll need if we practice that particular hobby for 14 years and become a world-renowned expert. That's the version we often get, and it's exactly what I did.

I bought a Martin® D1 acoustic guitar. This made my brother, a seasoned guitar player, cringe. The Martin is like the Ferrari of acoustic guitars.

It is a finely tuned piece of art. It is beautiful and pure sounding and was completely mangled in my hands for the 30 minutes I played it in our very short relationship.

I hated playing guitar and never touched it after that first time. It sat propped up against a chair in our living room in a black case, judging me every time I came home. "Hey, remember me? I thought we had something. You wanted to get serious. We were going to have something special together! What happened?"

I eventually sold that guitar on Craigslist® to a young woman who couldn't believe her good fortune. But it was a waste of money for me, and I lost in the transaction. I don't want you to do the same thing, so here are three hobby areas to be careful with:

1 | Cameras

No one dabbles with cameras. You either own a point-and-shoot or a piece of technology that would have wowed legend Ansel Adams.

Admit it—your friends couldn't tell you what half the features on their cameras actually do. Do you need a lens that could capture images from space to take pictures of your kids? Does your kid's soccer game really demand the same technology National Geographic® photographers capture monkeys with in Borneo?

2 | Hunting gear

Remember that time you went to Africa on safari and an elephant charged you? Yeah, me neither. But for some reason, lots of hunters own gear like they're octopuses, having at least eight guns for each of their imaginary arms. Now, clearly, you don't pick on people who own lots of firearms, but if you're going to invest in a sport that is truly beautiful and poetically strong, just make sure you're not the target of high-priced items you don't need. I don't want you to walk into that hobby "blind." (See me complimenting hunters and telling hunter-related jokes? Take it easy on me, guys.)

3 | Road bikes

As I type, someone is buying a road bike from Italy with about 17 vowels in the name. That's actually how you price road bikes. Each vowel in the name costs you about $400. Is there a more expensive mainstream hobby for you to get involved in? I don't think so. Maybe yachting, but so few of my friends are actively yachting these days. Down economy and all. Be careful buying a road bike. You know they don't come with pedals? That's like buying a keyboard without a *q*. I get it, I might buy a custom *q*, but I'd still like you to give me one just in case I need to type as soon as I get home from the store.

I hope this list saves you from an embarrassing Craigslist incident like the one I had with the acoustic guitar. But if it doesn't, at least mention me in the listing. Write, "$3,000 bike for sale. Jon Acuff said I didn't need it. Pedals not included."

IF A GIRLFRIEND TREATED YOU LIKE A CREDIT CARD DOES, YOU WOULD DUMP HER

Sometimes, we fail to see how horrible credit cards are for us because we don't look at them in the right context. We don't frame them the right way or break them down in a way that really spotlights how silly or outright crazy they are.

But recently, I had a thought. What if a girlfriend or boyfriend treated you like a credit card does? What if a credit card relationship were like a dating relationship? Once you look at Visa® the same way you look at that nightmare ex from your dark college years, you'll really start to see how bad credit cards are.

Here are a few examples of how a credit card would make for a horrible dating relationship.

1 | Getting rejected

What if, in the middle of a really expensive

dinner, at a fancy restaurant where the waiters wear white gloves and speak with British accents, your girlfriend unexpectedly denied you and left the date? That would be an uncomfortable situation, right? If she left with no warning and rudely rejected you in front of everyone, you would dump her.

2 | Your dating record

What if you had a really bad breakup with a girl, and for seven years the details of that breakup stayed on your "dating record"? Every time a new girl got to know you, she would say, "I like you, we have a lot in common, but why do you have such a low dating score? And what happened in Ohio in September of 2005"? That would be a bad dating situation.

3 | Phone calls

What if you forgot to call your boyfriend one night, even though you always called him like clockwork at the same time every night? And in response, he called you at work the next day, like 800 times? Then, what if he hired someone else, someone really, really mean and nasty, to collect on that missed phone call with threats and poisonous voice mails and threatening notes to your family made out of cut-up magazines? I doubt you'd have trouble letting that guy go.

4 | Selling the relationship

What if in the middle of your relationship, after years of dating, your girlfriend sold the relationship to someone else? You showed up on her front steps to pick her up for a date, and when the door opened, there was a burly guy with a mustache waiting for you. "Hi, I'm Frank. Your girlfriend sold your relationship to me. I'm from Wilmington, Delaware, and things are about to change." That would be a horrible dating relationship.

5 | Rewards

What if you had to perform crazy acts of loyalty and love for your girlfriend and all you got in return was not her love, but small, insignificant rewards? What if you planned an amazing night, cooked dinner, went on a horse-drawn carriage ride under the stars, spent thousands of dollars on the date, and at the end, your girlfriend gave you your choice of a clock radio or a subscription to *Golf* ® magazine? That would be weird. And bad.

Some of those comparisons are admittedly a bit extreme, but the truth is, most credit card relationships make the worst dating relationships look good. And if you pause long enough to think about what's really going on, it's easy to see that bad girlfriends, bad boyfriends and credit cards all deserve to be dumped.

WHEN ONE OF DAVE RAMSEY'S BLUE SHIRTS WEARS OUT, IS IT HUNG IN THE RAFTERS LIKE A JERSEY?

DAVE RAMSEY OWNS
SOME BLUE SHIRTS

I majored in journalism in college, so it's only natural that some of these chapters are hard-hitting. It only makes sense that while other books might take the easy way out and deal with the "softball issues," I'm going to dig deep and get to the real heart of the matter. I'll ask the tough questions, like the one you'll be dying to know once you get to week five of *Financial Peace University*. Put simply:

How many blue shirts does Dave own?

Every week, you see him in that blue button-down. Week after week, he rocks it. That might be the hardest-working shirt in America. Which begs the question, how many are there?

Is there only one shirt? Superman® never had a closet full of capes, and that's essentially what that shirt is. Dave is a superhero of financial proportions, battling debt and credit card Vikings at every turn. So is there only one cape?

And is it carved out of some sort of special material? Are the buttons titanium? Is it able to repel bullets, or at the very least, the spiteful glares of whole life insurance salespeople and FICO devotees?

Does he have a name for his shirt, similar to how you name your first car? Think about it—that shirt has traveled the world! Surely at some point, he's thought to himself, *Come on, old Blue, it's time for us to spread some hope.*

They say dogs can smell 10,000 more types of smell than we can; is it possible that Dave can see shades of blue the average human can't? Maybe they're all different, and I just don't have the visual palette to see the difference. I might see three blue shirts that look exactly the same, but Dave can actually tell that one is cornflower, one is cerulean, and one is periwinkle.

Let's imagine that the shirt isn't indestructible. How does he retire them when they wear out? Is there a ceremony? Like Larry Bird's jersey in the old Boston Garden stadium, does he raise it into the rafters in Nashville somewhere? Is there a parade of blue shirts hanging from the ceiling in his living room at home? Is there a wife on the planet who would be okay with that?

Let's say there really is more than one shirt. Maybe there are 17, and they each wait for their big moment on stage. It's like the shirt equivalent of getting called into the major leagues. It's go time! Do all the other shirts hate that one lucky shirt that got to be featured on the cover of *Financial Peace*? If I were a shirt, I probably would. I mean, this is what cotton dreams of when it's young.

When he buys them, do the cashiers think it's a little weird? Does he say, "I like this shirt. Do you have 16 more just like it?" If he owns a bunch of them, has he ever worn all of them at the same time? Just for fun, kind of like those inflatable sumo wrestling costumes people have at parties? Do he and Neil Cavuto from Fox News ever put on all their shirts at once and just sumo fight?

Have you ever thought about these types of questions while watching *Financial Peace University?* No? Oh. Yeah, me neither. That would be weird.

YOU NEED TO BABY-PROOF YOUR HOUSE FROM 27-YEAR-OLDS

Kids love electrical outlets. A lot of baby books won't tell you this, but it's true. They are drawn to the most dangerous things in your house like moths to a flame. Drawers full of steak knives, stairs, your Alaskan-crab fishing boat—kids always find the deadliest thing in your house and then try to play with it.

In response, you have to "baby-proof" your home. You plug the outlets and install incredibly annoying drawer locks on all your cabinetry. You put a gate up in front of your stairs. You get rid of your pet mongoose, Murray. It's a whole ordeal. But I'm here today to warn you about something you'll have to do later on in life as a parent. Something a little unexpected.

Eventually, you'll need to baby-proof your house from your 27-year-old.

You might not see it coming. When you send them off to college, you'll think that "off" is forever. They've left the nest. You cry a little, but this is what kids do. They grow up, and they go to college, or they join the military, or they get a job, or they do all three. And they're gone. There's a period on the end of that sentence. "They're gone." But more and more kids are coming back these days.

They're boomeranging right back into your house. So how do you lovingly prevent this? How do you baby-proof your house against a 27-year-old? We have a few ideas:

1 | Fill the basement.

The natural habitat of a 27-year-old when it comes to your house is the basement. One of the absolute best ways to baby-proof your home is to fill your basement with stuff. It doesn't have to be cluttered; it just has to have enough stuff that a bed can't be placed there comfortably. I personally find that treadmills really take up a lot of space while also providing an exercise option. Win-win.

2 | Start tea parties.

Your kids don't want to hang out with your friends. So if they even hint at moving back in, start having all your friends over for tea parties and card games and crafting nights. This will work even better if you can all wear big hats and constantly invite your 27-year-old to join you. "Sit down, sweetie! Tell us about your job search and your love life! Do you have a boyfriend yet?"

3 | Don't own a futon.

Your 27-year-old is drawn to a futon like a bear is drawn to honey. He can sense it in your living room from miles away, and given the chance, he will promptly turn it into a bed. Your best bet is to avoid all comfortable couches altogether. If you already own one, do what you do to keep the dog off the sofa while you're at work: put something heavy on it that he can't easily move to take a nap. Like a bookcase.

4 | Take dance lessons.

Most 27-year-olds don't want to see their parents dance all the time. It's embarrassing. If you're ready to take your baby-proofing to the next level, sign up for some dance lessons. I'm not talking about swing dancing—I'm suggesting tango. The idea of you and your wife practicing the tango in the living room will be like 27-year-old repellant. To really kick it up a notch, move all the furniture out of your dining room, hang a gigantic glass chandelier, and start referring to it as "The Ballroom." Forget them moving back in; you'll be lucky to see your kid at Thanksgiving and Christmas if holiday meals are served in The Ballroom.

5 | Install quarter machines on your laundry.

"Free laundry" is one of the first things 27-year-olds mention when they explain why they're moving home. Not at your house. You install some quarter machines and actually charge for laundry, and things are going to change—no pun intended. Want to really up your game? Install machines that only accept dollar coins. No one has those things.

If you're 27, please know that I'm not against you. How could I be? I was you for about a year, moving in with my parents back in Massachusetts after college. Eventually they pulled the ultimate trump card, though. They moved. Out of state. Eight hundred miles away.

Well played, Mom and Dad. Well played indeed.

WE NEED A NEW APP

Have you ever used the Shazam™ app for the iPhone®? I'm admittedly not that technical, but that thing is like magic. When you hear a song playing over the speakers at a restaurant, you can hold your iPhone in the air and Shazam will tell you exactly which song it is.

You can even hum a song and, in most cases, Shazam will figure out what it is and provide an easy link to more information. I feel like a caveman staring at fire whenever I use Shazam.

Fortunately, when it comes to money and making smart decisions with it, we've got the Ask Dave app. And although I'm not officially on the web development team at the Dave Ramsey headquarters, I do have a few ideas I'd like to add to the next version. Some of them are going to require scientific advances that eclipse the development of cold fusion, but I've met this team—they can do it.

Here's what I'd like an app to do:

1 | When you visit a store you've overspent at in the past, the app uses GPS coordinates to identify where you are and sends a text message to your accountability partner alerting them of the imminent shopping spree.

2 | Using Shazam-like technology, when the app hears a tempting radio commercial in the car, it starts playing loud, '80s-hair-band-heavy-metal music to block out the ad.

3 | Like a white blood cell attacking diseases in your body, this app would seek out and destroy other apps on your phone that cause you to spend more than you make.

4 | You could log all your possessions into the app. Then when you try to buy something you already have, it flashes a message saying, "Stupid tax! You don't need a new one of those!" on your phone.

5 | Whenever you face a tricky situation, you could shake the app and receive a "What would Dave do?" suggestion automatically.

6 | You could preset a car-dealer-pressure-cooker panic alarm that would go off in the middle of your tense conversation in the finance office to give you a quick exit.

7 | When the app hears the kind of music they play at high-end department stores, it starts a photo slide show of all the clothes you've bought but have only worn once.

8 | Using state-of-the-art photo recognition, this app would take a picture of a car and instantly tell you the total lifetime cost of leasing that vehicle. And then it would giggle a little, like Gizmo from *The Gremlins*.

9 | By detecting the magnetic strip on the back of credit cards, the app could find one in your wallet and growl like a timber wolf until you remove it.

10 | Somehow, the app would be able to focus all the energy of your phone into a small but powerful beam of light that is hot enough to melt your credit cards when you want to get rid of them.

11 | When you try to download other apps that aren't free, they have to meet your money app first. It would be like a high-school boy meeting the father of a girl he wants to date. The paid apps would have to prove themselves worthy of your phone.

12 | Using the barcode-scanning technology lots of phones offer, this app would scan something in and then immediately say out loud, "How are you going to pay for this?" You'd have 30 seconds to type in a suitable answer. If you've got the cash, the app would play a soft golf clap while you complete the purchase. If you don't have the money, the app would scream out, "Don't let me open a store credit card! Don't let me open a store credit card!" loud enough for everyone in the store to hear.

13 | Every morning, the app would wake you up with an alarm clock that says, "Good morning! You don't have a FICO score, and you're still alive! One more day of living the life FICO said wasn't possible!"

Is that too much to ask for in one app, or did I not ask for enough? I think it's possible, but then again, I think Shazam works via magic.

App developers, get on it. There's a whole world of us debt-hating weirdos who would love to add these features to the Ask Dave app.

YOU'RE GOING TO HAVE A MARRIAGE MONEY ARGUMENT

This is coming. Maybe you've always agreed with your spouse on every other issue in your marriage. Maybe you've had years, even decades of marital bliss usually only reserved for the end of movies on the Lifetime Channel. Maybe your love is so deep and rich that Hallmark has a line of cards inspired by your marriage. Maybe you're so in love you're able to hang wallpaper together, a silent killer of an experience that ends 82% of all marriages. But guess what?

When you start to whip your money into shape, you'll have an argument.

And that's okay. More than just okay, that can be the healthy, honest start to a new adventure for you and your spouse. But as you stand on this precipice, on the doorway to a shared experience that just might lead to more unity in your marriage

THERE ARE

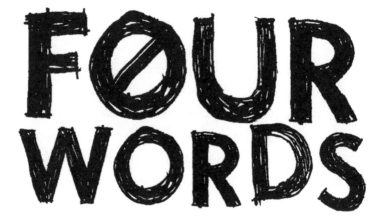

FOUR
WORDS

NO
SPOUSE
WANTS
TO HEAR.

than you thought possible, here are a few things to keep in mind:

1 | Never tell your spouse, "If you would just…"

No good comes of this phrase. I promise. You think it will, but it won't. Those are four words no spouse wants to hear. The problem is, "If you would just" is usually followed by a wildly exaggerated claim. For example, "If you would just stop buying shoes, we'd never have financial problems." Or, "If you would just stop playing golf all the time, we'd have all the money we ever needed." That's not true. There's no one magical step that will completely change all your finances at the drop of a hat. Be realistic (and kind) to your spouse, and never throw them under the bus with, "If you would just…"

2 | Don't pull a "marriage money sneak attack."

You've been reading some Dave Ramsey

books for a few weeks. You've been looking at your finances. You've been going over your checking account for hours at a time. And your husband hasn't. So when you say, "We need to talk," he's never going to see it coming. He's going to think you want to talk about where to go to dinner, not how to lay the groundwork for the next 40 years of your financial life. Guys, girls, husbands, wives, never pull a sneak attack. Give them a heads-up on what you'd like to talk about. They might not do their own research, but at least you've put the topic out there before you dissect it in your discussion. While you're thinking ahead, plan it out a few days in advance, get a babysitter, go out to dinner, and start the discussion. This won't be a one-night conversation; this is the start of a lifetime of change.

3 | **Sit down for the talk.**

If you ever find yourself in an argument

and you're physically in motion, the train has jumped the tracks. If you ever decide to have the money conversation while walking through the house and pointing out unused purses in closets or bass boats in garages, slow down. Nothing good comes from a conversation on the move—unless it's about the bear that's chasing you. At that point, run all you want.

4 | The marriage and money talk is a one-on-one conversation. Three's a crowd.

It's not a one-on-one about what your mom and your dad and the girl at work think you should be doing with your money. Keep this a couple thing, not a community thing just yet. You could always talk about your money with a counselor or a trained professional—the right third party can do wonders, but the wrong one can do damage. Keep it one-on-one at first.

5 | Don't throw a "conversation grenade."

I used to specialize in this move. I'd wait until my wife and I were about 15 minutes away from a dinner party, then I would bring up something serious we needed to talk about and drop it in the car like a grenade. After talking about it for a few minutes, we'd get to the party. I'd say, "I'm glad we had this discussion!" and roll out of the car while it was still moving (it's all in how you tuck your shoulder when you first hit the ground). Then later, when my wife wanted to continue the conversation, I'd say, "Oh, I thought we already talked about that." It's such a weasel move, it makes my teeth hurt a little.

Hopefully those tips will help when you and your spouse find yourselves on opposing sides in a money debate. But even more important than those tips is this simple truth:

YOU'RE NOT ALONE.

When you have a money argument, you might feel like you're the only couple who has these kinds of talks. You might feel like if you worked harder or had a better marriage, you'd never get into conversations like these. That's not true. The image of the couple that never disagrees about money is a myth. They've got naturally white teeth and breath that smells like cotton candy, and the only kind of fights they have are "hug fights," where they just hug each other over and over again. It's an idealized, Hollywood version of marriage, where "real life" never gets in the way of the love story.

Talking about money for the first time with your spouse might not be fun, but it doesn't have to be difficult. Here's to honest conversations that help you both get on—and stay on—the same page.

THERE IS AN ART TO PAYING WITH CASH

Dave Ramsey likes cash. Not in a Scrooge McDuck, swim-around-in-the-vault-of-bling kind of way, but more in the "shopping with cash is better" kind of way.

But if you grew up using a credit card or a check, it can be difficult sometimes to just jump into paying cash for everything you get. It feels different. It acts different. It causes different reactions when you pull it out.

So how do you do it? How do you know you're doing it right? How do you know you're really good at it?

Fortunately, I created a Karate-Like List Of Cash Purchase Qualifications, or "KLLOCPQ," if you prefer. Based on the martial arts system of awarding belts as different levels of skill are attained, the KLLOCPQ lays out the different degrees of expertise you can acquire when it comes to shopping with cash.

WHITE BELT | The Mention of Cash

When you're a rookie, a Daniel san if I may make a much-anticipated *Karate Kid* reference, you're probably ready to start off your journey by simply telling the salesperson you have cash. But you're not ready to flash it around like a Benjamin Franklin peacock.

YELLOW BELT | The Cash Flash

Saying you can pay in cash is one thing, but flashing it out? That's a whole different level, my friend. That takes someone with a little more experience. The first thing you have to master is the fan of your money. If you pull out a bunch of sweaty, crumpled up $100 bills, the impact of your action is severely reduced. You need to pull it out with a single, fluid motion, then fan it out as if through a David Copperfield bit of magic. That's why it's a yellow belt move.

BROWN BELT | Count It Out

A lot of people can pull money out in a dramatic fashion, but counting it out is a different beast altogether. You have to count it, so there's math involved. You also have to do it with flair, so there's drama involved. This is really where the sciences meet the arts. This is where form meets function. Go too fast, and each Benjamin won't get to shine. Go too slow, and you'll lose the salesperson's focus. Pace it right, and you'll get a great deal at that store.

BLACK BELT | Put the Money Back in Your Pocket

The threat of the money disappearing is every bit as important as it first appearing. Sometimes, salespeople are like the lyrics of an '80s hair-band power ballad—they "don't know what they've got 'til it's gone." And your job is to show them how quickly and easily that money can vanish. When you do the brown belt move and count it out, that money needs to be like a powerful buck, crashing through the woods. *Boom*, here it is! But when it's time to put it away, that money needs to be like a frightened baby deer: shy, quick to jump away when it senses danger. *Oh no*, high prices, no discount, this money is about to bounce!

There's a good chance that you will never see your money as a deer. I can understand that. I'm strange. But even so, don't be afraid to have fun with your cash purchases. You're not trying to take advantage of someone, but you do want to make sure you get a great deal. And if that means you have to go black belt from time to time when you go shopping, well then, so be it.

WRITING A BREAK-UP LETTER TO YOUR CREDIT CARDS

Five years after my wife and I read *The Total Money Makeover* and dumped our credit cards, we got a surprising letter from our credit card company. They hadn't heard from us in a while and just wanted to see how we were doing. They promised that they'd change if we took them back. Things would be different this time. If we'd only give them a second chance, we'd see.

After drying the tears of laughter that had streamed down my face, I realized why that letter was so funny to me. It was written like a scorned girlfriend or boyfriend. It literally read like someone I had dated who wanted to be back in my life. And that's when I had an idea—maybe I hadn't been clear enough in expressing my desire to never date that credit card again. Maybe there was still a door open that I needed to close once and for all.

Maybe we needed closure.

Thus, the invention of the "credit card break-up letter." Much like the form letters in the back of *Financial Peace*, this letter should be used as a tool—an awesome tool—to officially dump your credit card. Enjoy!

Dear (NAME OF CARD),

Wow, I don't really know where to begin. We've had some good times, haven't we? Remember that vacation I took you on? We had so much fun in (LOCATION). It wouldn't have been the same if you hadn't been there and had my back. And who can forget the time you helped me pay my (NAME OF BILL). That was a lifesaver!

But a few months later, I felt confused and hurt when you asked me for all that money back, plus 20% interest. I thought we had something special. I thought what we had was true. But now that I look back on it, for you, our entire relationship was about money. And it feels really one-sided. I give and I give and I give, and you just take, take, take. Sure, you give me small gifts here and there that you call "rewards," but even those I have to "earn."

I can't live this way. I feel like I don't even know you anymore. I want you out of my house, out of my life, and most importantly, out of my wallet.

I've found somebody else. Somebody I can trust. Somebody without hidden motives or hidden fees. He's simple but honest. Hardworking and true. I found someone who really cares about me and isn't into playing games.

I'm dating cash.

Don't call me anymore. I don't want you or your empty promises of frequent flyer miles. It's over.

Don't walk away mad. Just walk away, credit card… just walk away.

(YOUR NAME)

THERE IS NO MALE EQUIVALENT ❧ TO THE ❧ SPECIAL TORTURE that is the BRIDESMAID DRESS.

BRIDESMAID DRESSES: THE CRUELEST THING LADIES DO TO EACH OTHER

I live in Nashville, and right now, it's popular for hip guys to wear skinny lady jeans. I understand the appeal. They're cool and well-designed and look fun. I would wear them, I really would. The only reason I don't is, well, I'm a boy. I wear boy clothes. I think you can see my dilemma.

But despite being denied access to awesome lady jeans, being a boy does save me from one cruelty that is unique to women: the bridesmaid dress, a torture of which there is no male equivalent.

Sometimes people talk about the diamond cartel—that nefarious group of people who allegedly keep thousands and thousands of diamonds locked up so that the cost and demand stay high. The more I think about it, though, I don't think the diamond cartel has anything on the bridesmaid cartel.

Every woman in the world knows that a bridesmaid dress is a horrible torture to put on a friend. It's especially difficult when you've started to work on your money and beat debt. Out of nowhere, you get an invitation to spend $300 on a not-so-beautiful dress. And that's where the lying starts.

In fact, there are three very distinct lies ladies tell each other when it comes to bridesmaid dresses.

1 | You can wear this dress later.

That is the classic—the promise of future use that you can get out of the dress. The couture carrot that is dangled in front of you as your friend marches you toward an expensive dress you would normally never buy. As you fork over cash and look at your friend with frustration, she will tell you, "You can always wear it later." This is not true, ladies. Unless you are planning to mow the lawn in it or attend a "crazy bridesmaid dress party," there are few situations in life that demand an amethyst gown.

2 | You can cut it and wear it later.

Please tell me one instance in life when taking a pair of scissors to an item of clothing made it classier. Sure, everyone knows that jean shorts, or "jorts," offer increased mobility and catlike reflexes, but they're not classy. Other than a credit card, applying shears to anything rarely improves your lot in life. The only thing that happens less than a situation demanding an amethyst gown is a situation demanding an amethyst short dress. I promise. You're better off making the dress into a kite or a series of bandanas for some sort of tangerine-colored street gang you start in your neighborhood.

3 | My bridesmaids loved the dress I chose for them.

Stop—please just stop. Roughly 50% of brides

in the world believe that they have single-handedly ended the reign of ugly bridesmaid dresses. In their heart, they are convinced that unlike every other wedding in the history of mankind, their bridesmaids loved the dress she picked out. They didn't. They loved the bride so much that they pretended that they were okay with the dress. They loved the bride so much that they smiled as if a coral and lime strapless gown would work out just fine down the road as long as they took a pair of scissors to it.

I'm actually okay with bridesmaid dresses. The bride is the only one who is supposed to look beautiful. By definition, the bridesmaids are the silver medals of the day and shouldn't gleam as bright as the bride. It's her day! Plus, I'm not so crazy to go up against the bridesmaid cartel. They're good people. I like them. I think they do noble things. (If I ever wake up with a unicorn head in my bed, the bridesmaids' dainty equivalent of the mafia move, I'll know that my last-ditch efforts at compliments didn't work.)

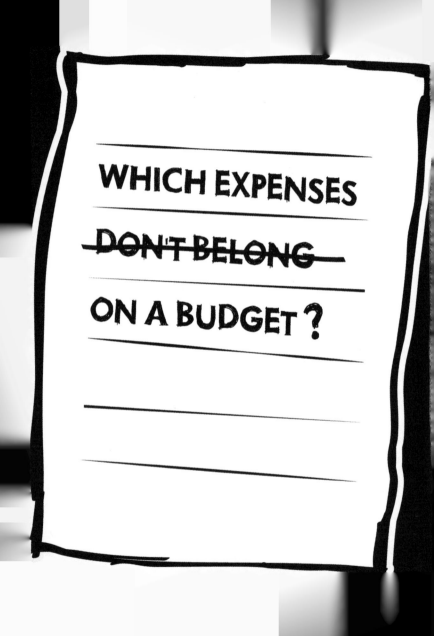

A COMPLETE LIST OF EVERY SINGLE EXPENSE YOU DON'T NEED TO WORRY ABOUT PUTTING ON YOUR MONTHLY BUDGET

PRACTICE YOUR
DEBT-FREE CALL
BY SCREAMING

"I'M DEBT
FREE"

AT FRIENDS
THE WEEK BEFORE.

4 WAYS TO MAKE A DEBT-FREE
CALL ON THE DAVE RAMSEY SHOW

You spent months, if not years, paying off your debt. You read the books. You used the envelopes. You were so gazelle intense that you kind of smell like the savanna. And now, you know what's next...

The debt-free phone call!

Long a tradition on *The Dave Ramsey Show*, thousands of people from across the country have called Dave over the years to scream, "I'm debt free!" It's one of the best parts of the radio show. We love it. You love it. It's the greatest.

But how do you make a really awesome call? You'd hate to spend a year paying off a student loan only to fumble the ball at the 1-yard line with a subpar debt-free phone call. Fear not, though. I'm here to help.

Here are the four steps you need to take in order to make a perfect debt-free call.

1 | **Practice on friends.**
A week before you plan on calling *The Dave Ramsey Show,* start practicing. Call random friends and then, without warning, scream as loud as you can, "I'm debt free!" Then hang up. Repeat as necessary.

2 | **Pick a safe place to do it.**
A lot of states have "no texting" laws that prevent you from texting and driving at the same time. There should probably be a "no debt-free yelling and driving" law as well. We'd hate for you to scream out, "I'm debt free," only to run into the back of a Porsche® and kiss your emergency fund goodbye. Pick a safe place to make your call.

3 | **Don't swear.**
We appreciate the colorfulness of the English

language as much as the next guy, but if you get all salty and/or blue during your call, there's going to be trouble. If you need to, swear a bunch right before you call *The Dave Ramsey Show* to get it all out of your system.

4 | Decide whether you'll do a countdown.
Studies have shown that 87% of all debt-free phone calls that jump the tracks are due to poor countdown management. Decide long before you make the call whether you'll actually do a countdown of 3-2-1 before you scream. Especially if you're calling with a spouse. Nothing derails a call faster than one spouse jumping the gun and yelling before the other one.

Hopefully, this little guide will give you the confidence and skills to make an amazing debt-free call. Take a deep breath, do some pre–phone call swears if need be, and let loose when you get on the phone.

LET'S NOT GET DISTRACTED BY
THE BRIGHT AND SHINY

The other day, my four-year-old, McRae, shared her thoughts on the pet situation at our house. Like many little girls, she and her sister, L.E., are desperate to own a cat that they can dress up like a princess and go on adventures with. But my wife, Jenny, is allergic. So alas, we will not be buying a cat anytime soon.

Pondering this sad reality, McRae remarked at dinner, "We can get a cat when Mom is dead." And although this is technically, scientifically true, I'm not sure we should tell Mom that when she dies, instead of a funeral, we're going to have a cat party. We'll just make it rain felines.

I've been thinking about cats a lot lately because of some credit card commercials I keep seeing. In the commercials, the announcer doesn't mention the rates or the responsibilities or the payments.

Instead, he just goes on and on about how you can customize the design of your credit card with photos of your family. You can put your kid's mug on the design. You can get a rainbow, even a double rainbow on the card if you so desire. The sky is the limit with the fun designs you can use to create your dream credit card.

But if you stop and think about that commercial for a second, you'll realize what they're doing to us. They're trying to distract us with the bright and shiny. They're trying to distract us with the colorful and playful. You know who else falls for that? You know who else gets distracted by the bright and shiny?

Cats.

Cats love lasers.

It's true. You can hypnotize a cat with a tiny laser or a colorful piece of yarn.

So when I talk to people about getting their finances in order and not falling for all the tricks of credit card companies, I'm not telling people they need to be financial experts. I don't want us to all win the Nobel Prize for our theories on economics.

I just want us to be smarter than cats.

Don't get distracted. Don't give in to the shiny. Together, I know that we can be smarter than cats. I believe in you and me.

COOL IS FICTIONAL

I invented cool.

Well, not the whole thing, but some of it. Okay, not even really "some," but more like one plant-based slang word in Boston. How?

I used to be what's called a "cool hunter" or a "trend reporter." There was a company that would pay me to track and reflect on trends. They'd then package them and sell them to clothing companies, cologne manufacturers and other purveyors of the hip.

One assignment was to send back any slang words we could think of. I reported a few that I was familiar with, but my list felt incomplete. It needed one more word. So, being the incredibly creative individual I am, I looked at the bright green aloe plant on my desk at home and came up with my own. I wrote a word down and because they wanted to see it used in a sentence, I did that too. Here is what I wrote:

Aloe = cool and sexy and fresh

Example sentence = "That girl has mad aloe."

A week later, the company sent out an email to all 1,000 influencers who worked for them. They called out one slang word they had received of the thousands that poured in from around the world. They highlighted one word that they were particularly excited about. Can you guess what word they loved the most?

Aloe.

The reason they did is that "cool" is completely fictional. We might think it's measurable or logical, but it's not. The things that are cool are completely made up. I didn't do anything special or unique in that moment. I did what cool people with cool ideas the world over have done for generations: I made something up.

The things we tend to think are cool are usually inconsequential gossamer. They are fluff and highly temporary, but we still think about them a lot. We still wonder if the people in our lives are cool by our definition of the word. More than that, we buy things based on how "cool" they'll make us feel.

Looking back on the seventh grade version of myself, Z. Cavaricci® pants were not that cool. For one thing, they had roughly 87 belt loops. They only came in colors like "baby throw-up," and they ballooned out like MC Hammer pants. (Don't you feel like we just had a wicked awesome '80s moment? No doy! Radical!)

But at the time, I thought they were the coolest things on the planet. I begged my parents for a pair, even though my dad was a pastor and we really didn't have money for Z. Cavariccis. I was certain that if I bought them, Sue in the eighth grade would think I was cool and date me.

Fortunately, my parents loved me too much to give in to my pants pleads. They refused to buy a pair. And yet I lived. I survived. I made it out of the seventh grade. Why?

Because cool is fictional.

CASH IS STILL KING,

BUT A DEBIT CARD CAN BE A **PRINCE** IN A PINCH.

THE SINGLE BEST ANSWER TO YOUR FRIENDS' QUESTIONS

Dave Ramsey tends to turn our friends and family members into storytellers.

When you tell them that you're reading *The Total Money Makeover* or going to a *Financial Peace University* class, they will inevitably tell you fanciful stories and reasons why they can't participate with you. Like a friend who refuses to get out of a bad dating relationship, they will spin yarn upon yarn about the cold, dark world that would await them should they ever get rid of their credit card.

"I'm a small business owner—I couldn't possibly get rid of my credit card."

"I travel a lot and couldn't rent cars without a credit card."

"Who wants to carry that much cash around?"

"What if I got into an emergency and needed some money right away? What if a shark bites my leg off and the hospital needs me to pay with a credit card before they'll reattach it? What then, huh? *What then?"*

And these are legitimate concerns—they are—but I'm going tell you how to answer all of them instantly. Not only will I tell you how to answer them, but I'll tell you how to respond in only two words. Just two words!

Ready? Ninety-eight percent of all fears about losing your credit card can be relieved with these two words:

Debit cards.

When we're afraid to get rid of our credit cards, we often forget the very existence of debit cards. We forget that a debit card is a like a smarter, nicer younger brother of a credit card. A debit card is like the kid from the small town that makes good, moves to the city, gets a college education, and then comes back home to take care of the community he grew up in.

A credit card? That's the older brother who got involved with some street youths, got into some trouble, and eventually became a thug. He probably wears a black leather jacket with a really mad tiger on the back.

But you're getting rid of your credit cards. You've already chopped them up with scissors. You've said farewell. And when friends and family members worry about you, about how you'll ever survive, don't forget to tell them these two words:

"Debit cards."

That's it, debit cards.

And if that's not enough, there's always the absolute best thing you can have when it comes to money, and that's money. Who knew? Who could have possibly foreseen the conclusion of this essay? Who could have predicted that cash would make a cameo? That far superior to credit cards, even better than a debit card, is cash? It's the backbone to your ability to use a debit card, the silent green friend who will always be on your side when you manage it, the single point of payment that scientifically causes you the most pause on purchases and thus the wisest decisions.

It's green. It's mean. It's the reason your debit card works in the first place.

No one puts cash in the corner. Not even a debit card.

NOT EVERYTHING IS AN EMERGENCY

When you start working through the Dave Ramsey materials, one of the first things you'll do is build up your beginner emergency fund. That's when you put $1,000 in the bank as fast as you can to cover those little emergencies that used to hit your credit cards. It's a simple step, but this little account is foundational to your long-term success with money.

But something funny happens once you realize you've got money in the bank. A lot of people have never had that kind of cash lying around. Even though you know it's only there for emergencies, even though you might have fought and clawed to pile up that money, your definition of "emergency" may start to get a bit… liberal.

You'll find yourself dipping into the emergency fund for things that aren't really emergencies. That's

A CARDIGAN **SWEATER** for a **DOG**

iS **NEVER** REALLY an **EMERGENCY.**

why we came up with this convenient checklist to help you identify an actual emergency.

15 ways to spot an emergency-fund-worthy emergency:

1 | If the emergency is that your car won't run unless you fix it, that's a real emergency.

2 | If the emergency is that your car won't bling unless you get some shiny rims, that's not a real emergency.

3 | If you've got an open wound, a femur bone jutting out at a disconcerting angle, or you can't see straight, that's a real emergency.

4 | If you've got skin that could be more bronze, that could glimmer with a deeper shade of awesome if you went to the tanning salon, that's not an emergency.

5 | If there are small, woodland creatures that are able to get into your house because of a gaping hole caused by a tree limb, that's an emergency.

6 | If you feel like the tile on the bottom of the pool could be a deeper shade of coral if you redid it, that's not an emergency.

7 | If the concern is that unless you buy this purse right now, you'll miss the two-for-one deal the store has running, that's not an emergency.

8 | If the emergency is that you won't be released from jail until you pay bail, go ahead and dip into that fund. You've got an emergency on your hands, my friend.

9 | If in describing the emergency, you use the phrase "out of style" to describe the item you want to replace, that's not an emergency.

10 | If the item you want to buy is some sort of clothing for a cat or dog, that's probably not an emergency.

11 | A "hair emergency" is rarely a real emergency.

12 | Unless your hair is actually on fire. That is indeed an emergency.

13 | A tooth emergency is almost always a real emergency. The phrase "home dentistry" should never be used in a sentence or acted upon in your living room.

14 | If the name of the thing you want to buy starts with a lowercase *i*, then it's probably not an emergency.

15 | If the remedy for your emergency includes the words "spa," "high-def," "country club," or "9- iron," that is not an emergency.

I, unfortunately, was able to write this list based on my own life. I once spent months explaining to my wife the emergency status of my need to buy a new laptop. (It will make me a better writer, the old one doesn't work well, etc.) When a new version would come out, I would raise the threat level to orange status and let her know our emergency was getting critical. I'd barter with her, "If I get a laptop, you can get _____." For some reason, she felt like buying two things we didn't need was twice as dumb as buying just one. Go figure.

A laptop is rarely an emergency. Fishing rods often don't reach emergency status. Leave the emergency fund alone. Save it for a rainy day. Not a really cute raincoat. Not everything in life is an emergency.

LIVE A LIFE OF "ENCORES"

I think the best part of a concert is usually the encore. It's like dessert at the end of a great meal. Just when you think things couldn't get any better… just when you're laughing and talking with friends about what a great show it was… Bono steps back onstage and sings an encore. It's the best!

It's the chance to enjoy something you love a second or even third time. In a culture that has become largely disposable, it's a reminder that some things are so good, they deserve another go-round.

That's why my wife and I always "encore" our kids' toys.

What's that, you say? What does it mean to encore a toy? I'm so glad you asked.

Every few months we edit the toys in our house. Our kids, like kids the world over, will get bored of a certain doll or board game. And so we'll

ENCORES

work great
for concerts & children's toys.

take it out of circulation. Like Disney® putting movies in "the vault," we'll put it in a closet for a few months.

Then, after our children have long forgotten about it, we'll encore that toy back into the house.

"Look at this game! Oh, we used to love it. Let's play again! This was so fun!"

We don't go so far as to wrap up the encore toys and present them as brand-new, but we definitely will bring something out for a reunion tour. It works like a charm. They've missed the toy and play with it again. And we save money instead of constantly buying new stuff to keep them engaged.

Kids aren't the only ones who fall for that either. I suspect that my wife is secretly encoring books I like to read. They often disappear and then reappear on the shelves in our house. Some I've read a dozen times; some I never even cracked after buying. But when they're encored, it's like they're brand-new again.

Don't be afraid to be like Bono at your house and encore a few things. I promise, you'll be surprised how much people love a good encore.

5 WAYS TO BEDAZZLE
YOUR ENVELOPES

If you've ever spent any time with the Dave Ramsey materials, then you know all about the envelope system. To summarize it: You build a budget, you pay all your bills on paper at the beginning of the month, and then you put the actual cash you're planning to spend on things like food, gas and entertainment in envelopes.

And fortunately, we've developed a pretty neat envelope system. It's convenient, durable and super easy to use. But maybe you wish it had a little more flair. Maybe you wish it had a little more flourish. Maybe you want to bedazzle it.

If that's the case, I have five ideas that might, in fact, change your world.

Five Ways To Bedazzle Your Envelopes

1 | Glitter

Although glitter is often referred to as the "crafting equivalent of rabbits" for its ability to multiply, don't quickly dismiss this option. Think about how fun it will be to pay your bills and grocery shop when you pull a glittery rainbow of an envelope out of your purse. Glimmer!

2 | Music

It's easy to find birthday cards that include a small audio file that plays when you open them. Buy one—with cash, of course—rip out the music player, and place it inside your envelope of choice. Imagine how great it will be to reach in for cash, only to be greeted with Kenny Loggins and the chorus to the song "Footloose"!

3 | Booby Traps

Having a hard time not blowing through your blow money on the first day of every month? I've got one word for you: scorpions. You put a scorpion in your envelope, and you'll really, really have to think twice before you'll be willing to open that envelope.

4 | Velvet

Nothing classes up a powerful piece of stationery like some velvet or velour. If you enrobe your envelopes in velvet, they'll step out of your pocket like your money is wearing a smoking jacket and just relaxing with the ladies. Classy!

5 | Bling

You want to really blow it up? Slap some fake diamonds on the envelope. Just slide a glue stick all over your envelope, then roll it around in a bunch of fake gems. In a matter of minutes, your envelope will go from "boring" to "Trump."

What's that, you say? Using the envelope system is about substance, not style? Form, not funtion? Financial responsibility, not flair? I'd love to talk with you about this, but my scorpion got loose in my car when I was enjoying some "Footloose." I've got to go take care of that.

THERE WILL BE BABIES

Visionary? Prognosticator? Sage? Though I generally deflect these titles of deep honor so as not to get too cocky, it's difficult when I am able to so accurately predict some things that are going to happen to you when you start beating debt.

I'm not going to predict one thing or even two—I've got three things I can *guarantee* will happen as soon as you start working on your finances.

1 | Everyone will get married.

Having been happily married myself for close to 10 years, I'd never call marriage a "virus," but every group of friends eventually goes through a matrimonial epidemic. Like a dam waiting to burst, the first friend who gets married inevitably sets off a tidal wave of "save the date" cards. Close friends, family

members—those are awesome weddings to go to. But the minute you start saving money and paying off bills, your mailman will invite you to his wedding. That waitress you love at your favorite restaurant in town? She asks you to *be* in the wedding. And though it's not technically a Baby Step, as we've already discussed, I think "Never buy a bridesmaid dress" should be.

2 | Everyone will have babies.

Just when you think you've escaped the onslaught of gift opportunities and you stop getting invited to weddings, your friends will start to have babies. Not just one or two— we're talking about entire fleets of babies. You'll think your friends are starting arena football teams, not families. And you'll get invited to baby showers where you have to buy gifts with names that sound like '80s tennis players, e.g. the baby Bjorn, or creatures from Avatar, e.g. the Bugaboo. Beware the baby shower, and remember—the kid won't know if you've re-gifted him a toaster oven you got at your wedding. What baby doesn't love toast?

3 | Everyone will buy a house.

Is there a more beguiling present than the "housewarming gift"? The house doesn't know you gave it a cutting board or some sort of decorative candle. The house never writes you a thank-you note. The house isn't particularly grateful. And yet, we go buy Fresh Cotton Yankee Candles® every time someone moves. I feel that if you've helped that person move—and you have if you own a pickup truck, which is apparently the universal sign for "I love helping people move"—you shouldn't have to buy them a housewarming gift. It's like a get-out-of-jail-free card. Am I comparing buying your friend a bottle of garlic-infused olive oil with going to jail? Yes, yes I am. A housewarming party is like some sort of gift jail.

I want to say right now that I forgive you if you don't invite me to your wedding, baby shower or housewarming party. We're still cool—I promise. But just don't be surprised when you buy Dave Ramsey's *The Total Money Makeover* and the very next day you get three wedding invitations in the mail.

Nothing good comes in yellow.

5 WAYS TO GET OUT OF A
HIGH-PRESSURE SALES SITUATION

I love salespeople. I think they can be some of the most helpful, knowledgeable folks on the planet. I used to be one and would never denigrate them. But there is something you need to know about them:

They are trained to sell you stuff.

Shocking, right? I know, I know, who'd have thought? When you're not in their store or dealership or business, they're training on the best ways to sell you stuff. They're reading books and going to conferences and basically doing everything they can to become the best at getting you to buy stuff.

And when it comes to shopping, we consumers never do the same thing.

Have you ever read a book on how to be a smart consumer? Have you ever gone to a "shopping conference" where you heard shopping experts share tips on making smart purchases? Have you ever received rewards and incentives to get even better at shopping?

Probably not. We don't think about shopping that way. So what happens is that we go into most shopping situations unprepared. The salesperson is like LeBron James. He's trained. He's made a living out of dunking on folks. And we just roll off the couch, straight into the game, and then act surprised when we buy something we really didn't want or can't afford.

Today, I want to level the playing field a little. I want to help give you a fighting chance. I want to train you on some simple ways you can get out of a high-pressure sales situation.

We've all been in those. We're standing with the salesperson on the model floor, looking at something we like, but we're just not sure we love it. And she's going through all her training, dropping jump shots and dunks all over the court. If we could just retreat for a day or two, we might have enough mental space to decide if we really can afford this. But the intensity is cranked up, and we feel stuck. How do you get out of that situation?

Here are five things you can say:

1 | **"I need to talk to my spouse first."**

Ahh, the classic "Throw your husband or wife under the bus" move. This is one of the oldest moves in the book, because it works. You're not saying you don't want to buy it; you just want to make sure your significant other is on board, too. If you're not married, then say you want to talk with a friend about it first or a relative. Don't budge on this, and you'll be fine. The only known sales side step is, "Wouldn't it be great to surprise your husband?" No, no it wouldn't. Your husband doesn't want to be surprised with a Kia® in the driveway, with a big red bow on it and a bill for $12,000.

2 | "This is tough because of the down economy."

Even if the economy is up and we're doing well, this is a great angle. Starting in the late 2000s, people started blaming the "down economy" for everything. It started with realistic things, like the struggle to find a job. But before long, folks were crediting the crab grass in their yard and failed dating relationships to the down economy. Tell the salesperson, "I would love to buy this today, but with the whole down economy thing…"

3 | "I never pay retail for anything. You'll have to do better than that."

Sometimes these are the magic words to unlock a previously unmentioned sale on the item in question. Just tell the salesperson that you've got a family rule, a boundary if you will, that you only buy things that are on sale. (And that should be true, by the way, because everything is on sale if you ask the right way.) If the item is already on sale, tweak it a little and say, "I only buy things that are on deep discount." Chances are, you'll be able to get them to drop the price even further.

4 | "Do you have this model in yellow?"

Unless you're looking at bananas, chances are the salesperson will not be able to immediately fulfill this yellow request. (And if you are buying bananas through a salesperson, where are you shopping? How many bananas are you going through in a week? So many questions.) Sure, you might not want it in yellow, but that's not what you said. You asked about a color option; there's nothing dishonest about that. And it gives you a chance to put the power back into your hand by taking the conversation from "You need to buy this thing you're looking at right now" to "I might buy something eventually if I really like it."

5 | **"Sometimes the summer rains remind me of how raindrops sounded on my grandfather's pond when we'd fish for big-mouth bass."**

That makes no sense at all. But eventually, if you talk enough gibberish, even the most persistent salesperson will bail on you and go talk to someone else.

That last one got away from me a little, didn't it? I'm not even sure what it means. But what I am sure of is that I want you to be prepared. I want you to be able to have a great game with the salesperson. One in which both of you win and you feel good about the whole thing.

Just don't buy the yellow model if they have it. So few things look good in yellow. Except for bananas.

EXTREME MAKEOVER, DAVE
RAMSEY STYLE

Dave Ramsey has ruined me for most reality television shows. Before Dave, I used to be able to watch reality TV without thinking about the financial consequences of the show. I could watch blissfully without questioning the foolish decisions people were making on *House Hunters International*®. I could laugh along with the hosts of remodeling shows as people went upside down on home renovations. But now? Now? I see price tags and debt.

And it's all Dave's fault. The biggest example of all is *Extreme Makeover: Home Edition*. On that show, ABC builds a brand new home for a family in need. Custom designed and tricked out to the max, the homes are always amazing. At the end of the show, the family stands behind a bus before they get to see the finished project. Then everyone

yells, "Move that bus!" and voila! Their new home is revealed.

Now, though, when I watch it, instead of cheering, "Move that bus!" I think to myself, *Pay those taxes, pay those taxes!* I know deep down, chances are the property taxes on that mansion are going to put a whupping on that family in the future. ("Put a whupping on" is a financial term—sorry for the jargon.)

But maybe it could be different. Maybe we wouldn't have those problems if Dave Ramsey created his own version of *Extreme Makeover: Home Edition*. What would that look like?

Six ways Extreme Makeover would be different if Dave Ramsey created it:

1 | At the start of each *Extreme Makeover: Home Edition*, the ABC crew shows up at someone's house and sketches their ideas for the house on a big piece of paper. With crayons. And smiley faces. Planning the home takes about

13 seconds of effort. Since Dave is far more realistic than that, and big projects, whether building a house or getting out of debt, are time-intensive, the planning wouldn't happen instantly. In fact, if I had to guess, the house would be built using a series of small actions, or "baby steps," if you will.

2 | Instead of those monochromatic t-shirts all the volunteers wear, every volunteer would wear a signature Dave Ramsey blue button-down shirt. Probably something in a periwinkle.

3 | Instead of a bus for the reveal, there would be a giant debt snowball that would have to be rolled out of the way. It would be the size of a tank, and the family would have to roll it away together as a final sign of the new life they're starting and the debt they're kissing goodbye.

4 | Instead of the wrecking ball, we'd start your demolition off by cutting all your credit cards in half. Instead of yelling at you with a bull-horn to wake up, we'd yell at you to bring your credit cards out.

5 | Instead of the participants on the show crying, credit card companies around the country would weep because one more person was escaping from debt. Title pawn places, preda-tory lenders—there would be a long list of people in bad suits, crying large, sad tears.

6 | In order to celebrate how you need "gazelle intensity" to get out of debt, we'd give you a herd of gazelles for your new backyard. We'd also give you a book on how to raise gazelles, so no worries there. It would probably be called *Total Gazelle Makeover.*

I'd watch that show. Especially to see how those gazelles adjust to suburbia. A giant snowball rolling down the street and a herd of gazelles prancing in the backyard? That's a reality television show winner right there.

What's funniest about that is where that belief comes from. Often, when we realize that we need to cut back on an area of our lives in order to really attack a huge debt snowball, we simply overreact. A spouse or friend mildly challenges our $50 weekly Starbucks® habit, and we instantly respond, "Great! So now you want me to sell my car and hand-make all my clothes! I'm so mad!"

That's not what Dave is saying at all. Not even a little bit. When I started going through *Financial Peace University*, I didn't trade in my Mac® laptop and start writing on brown paper grocery bags instead. Stuff is part of our life, and *managing* it does not mean *eliminating* it.

Sometimes, people go to extreme (and illegal) measures to save money. I heard someone call in on a radio station once and say that they wash out soda cups they find in the trash at the movies so they can get a free refill they didn't actually pay for.

If they called Dave with that story, I promise you he wouldn't say, "Great!"

He'd say, "Gross!"

Put the barrel down. Stop stealing apples from Old Man Johnson's farm. It's going to be all right. Dave doesn't want you to drive a burro.

YOUR KID WILL HATE DAVE RAMSEY

Thank goodness kids' hands are too small to hold bullhorns, and their attention spans are too short to organize well-funded protests. Otherwise, a sea of angry children would be marching upon Washington, D.C., right now. Why?

Kids hate Dave Ramsey.

Correction—some kids hate Dave Ramsey. What happens is that a parent gets a copy of one of Dave's books. They get plugged into beating debt. They get excited about it and really into what can happen not just for them, but for their whole family as they work together on saving money. And then, with little or no warning, they stop the gravy train that was running straight to their kids.

Allowances are fun to get. You receive them. They float into your life like a gift from a unicorn named Mom or Dad.

SOMETIMES KIDS

AND CATS

CATS

HATE DAVE RAMSEY.

Commissions are something you earn. And things you earn have to be worked for. With chores and tasks and—seriously, Dave Ramsey? I'm only 10! Why can't I just get some money now and then? Not only do I have to earn it, but I also have to save it and give it away? You are killing me, Dave Ramsey. You're like Cobra Commander® meets the Green Goblin® from Spider-Man®.

Your kids might not take it that personally, but trust me, getting your whole house in financial shape will impact everyone. The dog usually takes it pretty well, but if you go to generic pet food, the cat might have something to say about it.

Fight the good fight. The kids will thank you for it later. And let us know if you ever catch your kids with poster boards or a bullhorn. That protest is a matter of when, not if.

Have you ever bought something on your iPhone while you're in line buying something else?

THE FREE SPIRIT SCORECARD

According to Dave, there are ultimately two types of people in the financial world: nerds and free spirits. And although I've never danced with ribbons or worn any sort of glitter or clothing woven of flowers, it turns out I am definitely a free spirit.

Often in a marriage, as love and luck would have it, opposites attract. And when that attraction brings a free spirit together with a nerd, wild things can happen.

But how do you know which one you are? Without a personality test or taking some sort of profile study that discusses your natural strengths and gifts, who is to say which one you are?

That's why I have created two scorecards for you. In a matter of minutes, you'll know which side of the financial fence you fall on. You'll know who you are when it comes to cash and coins. And you'll be able to move forward with meeting and falling in love with the man or woman of your dreams. (I am unable at this exact time to guarantee that.)

Ready to find out if you're a free spirit?

1 | If you've ever said the phrase, "once-in-a-lifetime opportunity," while standing in the checkout line of a store. **= +1 POINT**

2 | You own clothes you've never worn. **= +2 POINTS PER OUTFIT**

3 | You've given a spouse a Christmas gift that was actually for you. **= +1 POINT** for each Christmas you did this.

4 | You tell people that you can tell the difference in the taste of different types of bottled water. **= +1 POINT**

5 | You have more credit cards than photos in your wallet or purse. **= + 1 POINT**

6 | The mall is like your version of the show *Cheers*. You're there so often, everyone knows your name. **= +1 POINT**

7 | You've ever referred to a car as "out of style." **= +1 POINT**

8 | If you've purchased something you didn't really understand how to use. **= +1 POINT**

9 | It caught on fire when you used it. **= +2 POINTS**

10 | If you've ever said, "But think of the memories we'll make," when trying to justify a purchase. **= +1 POINT**

11 | When you start a new hobby, you insist on buying the greatest version of that hobby's equipment (top-of-the-line tennis racket, golf shoes, etc.). **= +3 POINTS**

12 | When you don't use your credit card for a few days, the credit card company personally calls you and asks, "Is everything okay? We haven't heard from you in a while." **= +5 POINTS**

13 | You believe that "90-days-same-as-cash" is a great deal. **= +2 POINTS**

14 | You've ever purchased something because of "all the frequent flyer miles you'll earn." **= +2 POINTS**

15 | Black Friday, the shopping day after Thanksgiving, is considered a national holiday around your house. **= +2 POINTS**

16 | You've bought something on your iPhone while you're in line buying something else. **= +1 POINT**

17 | You've cried while watching a television commercial. **= +2 POINTS**

18 | Your retirement plan is to win the lottery when you're in your 60s. = **+6 POINTS**

19 | Your "blow" envelope is constantly attacking your other envelopes, like a wolf among sheep. **= +2 POINTS**

20 | You buy and wrap more gifts for yourself than other people actually give you at Christmas. **= +2 POINTS**

21 | You've ever written, "I'm so mad at Dave Ramsey!" in the margins of one of his books. **= +3 POINTS**

22 | "Dave" is now considered a four-letter word around your house. **= +6 POINTS**

23 | You feel like "cash-back bonuses" from credit card companies are like the "tooth fairy for adults." **= +5 POINTS**

24 | In your mind, the offensive, horrible-to-say-out-loud "b-word" is "budget." **= +3 POINTS**

25 | You celebrate your "half birthday" and expect gifts. In your 40s. **= +2 POINTS**

26 | The first time you held *Financial Peace* in your hands, it burned a little, like a vampire touching garlic. **= +10 POINTS**

27 | You own more books that you haven't read than books you have read. **= +2 POINTS**

28 | You've ever spent the night in a store parking lot to be the first one through the doors on big sale days. **= +2 POINTS**

29 | You knocked someone down when the doors finally opened. **= +1 POINT** for each person you knocked down; **+3 POINTS** if you stepped on them a little as you walked in.

30 | When people in your neighborhood talk about "keeping up with the Joneses," they are referring to you. **= +2 POINTS**

31 | Your dog has more clothes than most small children. **= +2 POINTS**

Now that you've looked through all the different questions, tally up your score and see where you fit.

0–10 POINTS | Nerd

I mean that in the nicest possible way. You're not a free spirit. Your skin might have even crawled a little reading through these ideas. You're a nerd. The question now is, how much of a nerd are you? Try the Nerd Scorecard (on page 121) and get your answer!

11–20 POINTS | Shopper

It might not be your hobby or even your passion, but you're no stranger to a shopping spree. You know your way around the mall and even have a small list of online sites you like to order from. You've got a budget, but you can't remember the last time you actually looked at it. Was it in the office or the kitchen? It's definitely in one of those two places.

21–40 POINTS | Bling Bomber

You might not be a rapper, but when you shop, you "make it rain." The word *sale* drives you into a hummingbird-like sugar craze. Budgets are for people who don't live in the now or really seize the day. You've got to spend money to make money!

41+ POINTS | Free Spirit

You are shopping right now. Even as you read this, you are shopping online and might even be on the phone, checking on something you ordered. You've said, "I want to buy that car next," while sitting in the finance office of a dealership, signing the papers for the new car you just bought. Budgets are for boring people.

the PET STORE

is a "FREE ZOO."

THE NERD SCORECARD

When I was growing up, the term *nerd* was not a compliment. Long before programmers and young CEOs of internet companies reinvented that word, *nerd* meant something entirely different. And I should know, because in some ways, I was one.

I collected comic books.

I read *The Lord of the Rings* constantly.

I wore suspenders to the eighth-grade dance.

But despite my humble, Urkel-like upbringing, it turns out I'm not a nerd in the Dave Ramsey sense of the word. I'm not the brains behind the budget, the math behind the investments, the stats behind the calculations. I don't crunch numbers for fun, I can stand when things are out of place, and I scored incredibly low on this scorecard.

How about you? Are you a nerd or a free spirit? Let's find out with this helpful Nerd Scorecard:

1 | You were glad recycling got all popular, because you've been reusing things for years. **= +1 POINT**

2 | You use the phrase "perfectly good" a lot. As in, "What's wrong with these paper towels? They were only used once. They're perfectly good." **= +1 POINT** for each time you've said it in the last week.

3 | When a spouse won't listen to you, you throw Dave under the bus and say, "Well, Dave Ramsey says…" **= +2 POINTS**

4 | You consider doing the budget on a Friday night with a little light jazz in the background a hot date. **= +2 POINTS**

5 | You don't call your clothes old and worn-out; you call them "vintage." **= +2 POINTS**

6 | You taught yourself how to cut your own hair. **= +1 POINT**

7 | You're not very good at it. **= +2 POINTS**

8 | Others have definitely noticed you're not very good at it, but now that it's out there, you can't bring yourself to actually pay for a haircut ever again. **= +3 POINTS**

9 | You ask the waiter to wrap up the free bread at restaurants as if that is part of the doggy bag. **= +2 POINTS**

10 | You don't use Sweet'N Low®, but you have been known to pocket a handful at a diner, "just in case." **= +2 POINTS**

11 | You quickly smooth out wrapping paper when people open gifts at Christmas so that you can use it again. **= +2 POINTS**

12 | You consider expiration dates on milk a suggestion, not a rule. **= +2 POINTS**

13 | The first time you picked up *Financial Peace*, you cradled it and said softly, "Where have you been all my life?" **= +2 POINTS**

14 | The only part of *Financial Peace* you disagreed with is where it talks about actually spending your money. **= +2 POINTS**

15 | You consider the library a "free bookstore." **= +1 POINT**

16 | You consider the pet store a "free zoo." **= +1 POINT**

17 | You consider the lobster tank at grocery stores a "free aquarium." **= +2 POINTS**

18 | Every now and then you "edit" your kids' toy box, remove some toys for a few months, then bring them back out later, as if they are new. **= +2 POINTS**

19 | You've tried to do that same thing with your wife's shoes or husband's fishing rods. **= +4 POINTS**

20 | You like jury duty because of the free lunch. **= +2 POINTS**

21 | You don't buy Valentine's gifts because it's a holiday invented by the gift-card industry. **= +1 POINT**

22 | You don't buy deodorant because it's just a scam invented by the deodorant industry. **= +2 POINTS**

23 | You cut coupons so often, you had to get industrial-strength, Dave Ramsey–sized scissors. **= +2 POINTS**

24 | You love cutting coupons so much, you named your scissors. **= +3 POINTS**

25 | You once made a grown man cry while negotiating a car purchase. **= +4 POINTS**

Now that you've looked through all the different questions, tally up your score and see where you fit.

0–10 POINTS | Free Spirit

If you could have scored a negative, you would have. You're not a nerd. You're a free spirit, prone to shopping sprees and "Forget about the budget— let's just live!" moments. Try the Free Spirit Scorecard to see what your real score is.

11–20 POINTS | Nerd-ish

You're not ready to be the weird lady raising chickens in a downtown apartment for the free eggs, but you're making a lot more budget-based decisions than most people. You balance your checkbook regularly, shop only when things are on sale, and you got rid of your credit cards years ago.

21–40 POINTS | Coupon Commando

You can smell discounts like squirrels smell nuts. You don't carry a calculator for crunching numbers, you have a custom-made holster for it that you wear like a gunslinger. You got that holster on sale. When it comes to budgets and paying down debt, all you do is win.

40+ POINTS | Nerd

Every friend you have comes to you for money questions. When you were a child, your parents gave you an abacus for Christmas. You can't hit a curveball, but you can mathematically predict the odds of the pitcher throwing one. You are a nerd to the tenth degree. Or pi, as it were.

cutting up **CREDIT** **CARDS** in front of friends is a **GREAT** conversation starter.

TELLING FRIENDS
ABOUT DAVE RAMSEY

When we experience good things in life, we want to share them with our friends and family members. When we see a funny movie, we look over in the theater to see if our friend is laughing, too. When we give a relative a gift, we watch their face to see if they like it. We like to share and pass along the good things in our life. And that certainly holds true with the Dave Ramsey materials.

When you read *The Total Money Makeover* or take a *Financial Peace University* class, it's only natural to want to tell people about the experience. But what's the best way to do that? You don't want to just hand them a book and say, "Hey, you know how you're all dumb and stuff with money? Well, this will fix you. Get reading."

You need some tact, some finesse. And fortunately, that's my middle name—it's actually

Jon Finesse Acuff. So here are four smooth ways to tell friends and family members about Dave Ramsey.

1 | Leave an FPU CD in your car stereo.

Have it playing when you pick up a friend for a night out to dinner. Oh, what's this we're listening to? I'm glad you asked. It's actually a financial experience I recently had that changed my life, and…

2 | Constantly cut up credit cards in front of friends.

Wait until they come over to hang out, then pick up your Dave-sized scissors. Grab a stack of your old credit cards and start chopping away as if that's a perfectly natural thing to be doing. "This? Oh, these are just some old credit cards. Just chopping them up. Doing what I do!"

3 | Get caught by surprise.

Right before friends come over for dinner,

put in a *Financial Peace University* DVD. Leave the front door open, and as they walk in, you can act surprised that they are there. "Whoa, I was right in the middle of watching this. Go ahead and pull up a chair."

4 | Flip your car upside down. Temporarily.

What better way to illustrate the dangers of having a car payment that leaves you up-side down than actually having your car upside down? Temporarily. Look for a *Dukes of Hazzard®*-sized dirt mound inexplicably located in the middle of the road. Jump it. Flip the car in mid-air and immediately say, "This is dangerous, but not as dangerous as having your car payments get you upside down." Then land the car safely and hand them a copy of *The Total Money Makeover*.

Okay, the guys in suits have told me I can't technically encourage you to launch your car over dirt mounds. Fair enough, but if you do want to share the Dave Ramsey materials with your friends and family members, we encourage you to just be honest. Share what you like, share what you're learning, share what's different about your finances.

You don't have to be crazy or extreme. Just be real. And right-side up.

THE GENEROSITY OF FUTURE ME

Morning me used to hate night me. That's a bizarre sentence, but it's true. Night me was such a party animal. He'd stay up late, watching horrible reality television shows and reading books into the wee hours of the morning. And then morning me would get up, ready to take over his shift, only to find that he was completely exhausted.

"Come on, you stayed up all night again? How am I supposed to go to work and take care of the day like an adult? Dang you, night Jon, you are such a punk!"

Okay, that conversation didn't really happen. Although it feels like it, there are not really two versions of me. The same guy who stays up late is the same guy who gets up in the morning. It would be silly to pretend there are two different people working the same day under the same name, Jon

Acuff, but you'd be surprised how many people do that when it comes to money.

Especially in regards to the *g* word.

I'm talking about giving. When you get gazelle intense with beating debt, sometimes it's easy to make the mistake of thinking that giving is something that will come later. And when we talk about later, it's fun to imagine how generous future me is going to be.

"Right now, giving doesn't really fit into the plan. But in the future? Down the road? I'm going to be like Bill Gates! I'll probably just rent a hot-air balloon and drop stacks of cash out of it. I'll play Natasha Bedingfield music as I do, just to get people dancing and really enjoying the full depth of my amazing generosity. Gonna change the world, man, really change the world."

But you know the truth about "future me"? He or she is incredibly slippery. Just when you think the future has finally arrived, something else comes up. Something more important or critical or… well, I can start giving later.

Later is a make-believe land that never comes. Future me is a make-believe person who never really gives.

You want to really get gazelle intense? Want to beat debt and have long-term success with everything Dave Ramsey talks about?

Say good-night to future me. Start giving today. Budget some giving right now. You don't have to go crazy, but planning for your tithe to the church or even for a little extra tip money for a struggling, single-mom waitress won't melt your debt snowball. Giving is important no matter where you are in the Baby Steps; that's why Dave put it at the top of his budget form!

In fact, the joy you feel from giving even a little today might be the extra push you need to really get out of debt as soon as possible! The truth is, future me won't know how to be generous with a lot unless present me learns how to be generous with a little.

So, give a little.

DECIDING WHICH TYPE OF DEBT-FREE CALLER YOU'LL BE

We've already discussed the four steps you might need to take when it's time to call in and yell, "I'm debt free" on *The Dave Ramsey Show*. The steps are simple, and the plan is easy. The final decision you need to make, though, is this: "What type of caller will I be?"

All callers are not created equal. In fact, there are six common types that we hear on the show.

See if you identify with any of these:

1 | The Spouse Superstar

Sometimes, married couples will call in to talk to Dave at the same time. In theory, this should be a lovely example of marital communication, as each spouse shares the call and both get to talk. Consider it like a

verbal tag-team wrestling match. When one person stops talking, the other person starts talking. What sometimes happens, though, is that a "Spouse Superstar" emerges. Instead of sharing the spotlight with their loved one, a husband or wife will dominate the entire phone call, never letting their spouse chime in. At every turn, they cut their partner off until at long last, the listening audience kind of forgets there was someone else on the phone.

2 | The Scream Machine

On the best calls, when it's time to say, "I'm debt free!" the person screams as loud as they can. On the wildest calls, we face what we call a "Scream Machine." Instead of having a normal conversation until it's time to yell, "We're debt free!" Scream Machines just yell the entire conversation. THEY CAN'T HELP IT! IT'S SO EXCITING! THEY HAVE TO YELL THE WHOLE TIME!

3 | The Debt Whisperer

The polar opposite of the Scream Machine, this person quietly and slowly talks about their debt experience. You can't really tell if they are talking or if a tiny fall breeze is blowing through some river birch trees. Turn up the radio all you want; this caller is like a gentle bubbling stream that softly says, "*Psst. I'm debt free.*"

4 | The Explainer

Details. Details. Details. Batten down the hatches, my friend, you're about to be awash in an ocean of details. And this is probably how I would make the call, unless my wife was within arm's reach and could pinch me. I want to talk. I want to over-explain. You see, there was this day where I found a soda can that was worth a nickel, and so I returned it, and I took that nickel and then brought it to the bank and used it as part of my debt snowball. Only I wasn't ready to put that nickel in my debt snowball once I got to the bank, so I called my wife and I talked to her about it for a while, and we collectively decided that…

5 | The Word Kidnapper

You're not going to get 12 words out of this person. Dave will ask questions. He will poke and pry for hours, and every question he asks will be answered with one-word responses. "So you found yourself upside down in a car. Was that a difficult situation to get out of?" Dave asks. The response: "Yeah." It's as if the Word Kidnapper is holding words hostage and will only release them one at a time after a period of tense negotiating.

6 | The Multi-Tasker

We are a busy culture. We like to do more than one thing at a time. Same goes with the phone calls we make to Dave Ramsey sometimes. The Multi-Tasker calls up and then proceeds to have a conversation with someone they are sitting next to, while driving around on errands, and possibly filing taxes. The Multi-Tasker is busy, and as fun as it is to be on the radio, it's only one of many things on their to-do list.

I don't know if you'll fit one of these stereotypes, but as I confessed, I'm probably an Explainer. I'd probably talk your ear off if you were Dave Ramsey. I wouldn't mean to, it's just that I got $3.52 back when I returned some socks at Gap®, and I used that money to apply to my debt snowball and when I did, I realized that I was moving through the Baby Steps pretty quickly, and...

A CREDIT CARD IS A CREDIT CARD
IS A CREDIT CARD

Dave Ramsey has ruined me for credit cards. Not just using credit cards. He's certainly changed that part of my life. Even when I pull out my debit card, I feel a little weird. I don't exactly feel crazy, but at least a smidge odd.

He's even ruined my ability to see credit card advertisements and not laugh out loud. I blame him for that. I used to be able to watch television, see an ad for a credit card, and not think twice about it. Now? What happens when I see them? I really watch them. I don't casually let them float by the screen—I listen to what they're saying and then talk back to the television like an over-excited crowd watching a horror movie.

I see a spot in which a couple talks about booking a vacation with a credit card so that they can earn miles, and in my chair at home I yell,

"Don't do it! Don't go on that vacation. Don't open that door! There are killer fees waiting inside. You'll never be able to redeem those miles. Noooo!"

And when I'm not yelling at the television, I'm picking apart what's being said in the ad. One of my favorite things credit card companies do is criticize other credit card companies.

There's an ad I've seen recently where the commercial talks about how horrible the customer service is if you do business with their competitor. Other commercials warn you about the high fees and jacked-up rates their competitors offer. "We're the good guys, not like our competitors. They just want your money. We're not about that. We're different. We're not like everyone else."

If you've spent seven seconds with Dave Ramsey and his materials, though, you know that a credit card is a credit card is a credit card. In the world of credit card marketing, there are not good guys and bad guys. There's not one credit card company who wants your money and another who wants your hugs and just hopes to see you follow your dreams with everything you've got.

Put in even simpler terms: A credit card company criticizing another credit card company is like a hammerhead shark talking trash about a great white shark. In that scenario, you still get bitten.

There's not a shark victim on the planet who says, "You know, a shark took my leg. Ripped it clean off my body, but I'm not mad. It was a tiger shark, not a mako, and that makes all the difference in the world."

A shark is a shark. A credit card is a credit card. When they're telling you they're not, be very careful. At that point, they're already circling.

THE PRE-DAVE RAMSEY
SHOPPING SPREE

I have a terrible confession to make. Oh, the shame —the shame!

Right before my wife and I decided to read *The Total Money Makeover*, we did something that I am not proud of. The day before we started reading the book, we agreed that before we did, we should buy a bunch of stuff we like.

We were afraid that as soon as we read the book and listened to *The Dave Ramsey Show*, we'd never be able to buy fun stuff again. Dave would put a chokehold on my fun, and I'd never get to go to the mall again. So like a hamster gathering nuts in his cheeks for a long journey, I wanted to grab everything I could and clutch it close to my heart.

New iPhone? Yes, let's do it.

New laptop? Of course!

New sneakers? Why not!

I wanted it all. There was no limit to my purchases as I happily enjoyed a pretty sweet pre–Dave Ramsey Shopping Spree. But here are the two problems with that approach to things:

1 | Dave Ramsey never says you can't buy things.

That's just silly. Dave wants you to save and invest and get out of debt. He never said anything about not owning an iPad or not being able to get new shoes. Buy as many as you like; just use cash, get a good deal, and plan for the expense.

2 | It's dumb to dig a deeper hole before you start working on your money.

I wouldn't go to a crazy buffet the day before I started a diet. I wouldn't begin a marathon five miles away from the starting line. I don't want to sabotage my success in any other avenue of life, so why do I want to start my road to Financial Peace even further away from my goal?

Don't be your own worst enemy when it comes to beating debt. Don't dig fresh pitfalls in your path before you start walking. Don't add unnecessary miles to the mountain you're going to climb.

Down with the pre–Dave Ramsey Shopping Spree!

Long live being smart before, during and after you read *The Total Money Makeover*.

THERE'S NO SUCH THING AS A
5-STAR BABY STROLLER

When I was a kid, I'm pretty sure my parents didn't have a fancy baby stroller. They just strapped me onto a small shopping cart with a piece of rope and pushed me around. If it fell over, so did I. If it got hot out, so did I. If I got thirsty, I had to wait until the heavens opened up and sent the dry earth some rain.

But now? Times have changed for baby strollers. They've got cup holders and shades and emergency brakes and side curtain airbags. They have more technology in them than Ford's® first Model T did. Some are sporty and light, able to fold down into next to nothing like a Transformer. Some are thick like tanks and designed for off-road pushing. Some are luxurious and covered with soft baby amenities. But as many different features as they offer, as many different options as they present, do you know what trait they all share?

Every baby stroller is safe.

When you become a new parent, you might not think so. You might think that more money equals more safety. You might think, "I don't want to skimp on my child and buy her something that's dangerous. What kind of bad parent would do that? To be the best parent I can possibly be, I've got to spend outside of my budget. This is my kid we're talking about!"

And that is an admirable desire. That drive to be the best parent you can be comes from an honest, noble place in your heart. But where it gets twisted—where it gets all tangled up—is where you start to believe that spending more money on your child makes you a better parent.

You see this logic first start to manifest itself with strollers and cribs. That's not to say that some strollers aren't nicer than others. Some are more comfortable. Some cribs are easier to put together or have bars that slide down without pinching your fingers in the middle of the night. There are a million features that separate a cost-efficient baby item from an expensive one. But you know what feature doesn't?

Safety.

When the agencies that deem products safe or unsafe look at strollers, they don't look at the price tags before they begin their evaluations. They don't say, "Well, this stroller costs half as much as this other one, so they only need to be half as safe." They don't say, "This one costs twice as much as this other one; let's make sure it's twice as safe."

There's not one safety standard for cheap products and a different one for expensive products. There's not a high-end seal of approval and a budget-based seal of approval. Last I checked, J.D. Power didn't have a five-star safety rating for strollers or cribs.

Baby strollers either measure up to one consistent set of safety standards or they don't. You're not keeping your child dramatically safer with each dollar you spend. Cooler? Sure. What toddler doesn't want some sort of ridiculous whip sitting on dubs they can roll up to playgroup in? What baby doesn't want the Maybach® of strollers, complete with dual climate zones for when big brother decides to hop in? What three-year-old doesn't want a diamond-encrusted sippy cup for his vitamin-infused pomegranate juice?

Dare to dream, kids, dare to dream.

But parents, don't buy the lie that to be a good mom or dad you have to spend more money than other parents. That's just not true.

DO YOU HAVE TO WEAR A

BURLAP SACK

TO A

FINANCIAL PEACE UNIVERSITY

CLASS?

YOUR FIRST NIGHT AT
FINANCIAL PEACE UNIVERSITY

It's your first night at *Financial Peace University* (FPU). You've got all your class materials, your pen and a great attitude. Now, the most difficult question of all, what do you wear?

Is it weird to dress up in expensive clothes for a class about being smart with your money? Should you dress down for a class about saving and investing your cash? Will people be able to tell your clothes were purchased with credit cards?

Good questions, and I suggest you play it safe and wear something in burlap.

A lot of people will tell you that burlap makes for an uncomfortable shirt, but what do they know? It's difficult, with such short notice, to find a humble barrel with rope suspenders to wear to *Financial Peace University*. But that might be over-the-top. Aim to wear something that says, "Hi, how's everyone doing? Nothing to see here; please don't do the mental math of how much my outfit cost. Let's focus on the FPU material tonight!"

Your purse and shoes should probably also not end in an *i*. Gucci®, Armani®, Fendi®, I'm talking to you. Go with flat shoes, as in, "I'm flat serious about this new budget. Let's do it!"

And guys, leave the designer jeans at home. Aim to wear denim that sounds like something a debt-free cowboy would own. Think "hustler" or "rustler," or "cattle-drive jeans." Okay, I made up that last one, but I just want to make sure you're thinking mesquite enough.

If you have a car you've leased, or as Dave says, "fleeced," don't drive it that first night. The FPU boxes that the materials come in can detect leased cars and will probably hurl themselves at you as you enter the room.

Or you could go to a group where no one is ridiculous like this. A group that's full of folks just like you, working hard to get their money under control, and more focused on what really matters. Not burlap shirts. I mean, both approaches are pretty good options when you think about it, but you'll probably want that last one.

CHRISTMAS
FALLS IN
DECEMBER
THIS YEAR.

ember

FRI

SAT

AGAIN.

SOME SURPRISES AREN'T
REALLY SURPRISES

I used to work in the marketing department of one of the largest retail store chains in the country, if not the world. We were a well-oiled machine of efficiency, producing millions of pages of catalogs and newspaper advertisements every year. There was nothing that our team of experts couldn't handle.

Except for Christmas.

Every September, after months of pretending the year was not barreling away from us day by day, we'd look at the calendar and exclaim, "Wait, Christmas is in December this year! Oh no, we're not ready!"

Each year, we acted like Christmas was a surprise, like it was a constantly moving target. "Is it in May this year? Didn't it hit in October last year? Check the calendar! I think the government moved it to spring this year!"

We had all the warning in the world. When we got back from Christmas vacation, we could pretty much estimate that we had about a year before it hit again. But by pretending we were surprised by the date, we made ourselves feel a little better about being unprepared for the work we had to do.

Sometimes we do that exact same thing with our money. We come up with a budget, and we're happy with it. We don't see any problems with finishing the month with enough money. But all of the sudden, we run into a "surprise." Are we really celebrating our daughter's birthday this month? With presents? That we buy? I have be honest with you, I didn't see her birthday coming.

But it's not just holidays that sneak up on us. Here are a few things that you can't claim are surprises when it comes to budgeting.

1 | Cars break down.

That's not an "if," that's a "when." No matter what *Consumer Reports*® says, every vehicle ever made has a 100% chance of falling apart—in time. That's what they do. So if your budget doesn't have room for car repairs, you're setting yourself up for an unenjoyable "surprise."

2 | College textbooks are expensive.

Based on the cost, it's safe to assume that college textbooks are printed on gold leaf and endangered baby seal skins. So when your kids head to college, don't be surprised when the cost of books and a whole list of other things comes up.

3 | Air conditioners fall apart.

Or hot water heaters. Or garbage disposals. Or a million other things that come with owning a home. Your house might have a longer vitality rate than your car, but it's not perfect. Roofs only last so long. Pipes burst. You'll wake up one morning and your kitchen cabinets will be ugly. You'll swear they weren't when you went to bed, but there's the evidence right there. Ugly cabinets. Home costs aren't really a surprise.

4 | Christmas is on December 25.

Even though the introduction was about this, our favorite December holiday causes more "surprises" than anything else. This is the time of year when we find our money scampering away from our wallets and purses like frightened otters. When we find ourselves needing to buy gifts for coworkers and schoolteachers and neighbors and—whoa, we haven't even talked about our family yet. Even if you play it tame on Christmas, you're still going to have a lot of people on your "gift list." Christmas is not a surprise.

Surprises are like tiny grenades for budgets and Financial Peace. They'll come up sometimes. You'll get blindsided by them from time to time, but here's the trick:

Never get surprised by the same thing twice.

When a financial stunner hits you for the first time, write it down in your journal or your budget, and start a new envelope for that thing. Promise yourself and your spouse or accountability partner that you'll never get blindsided like that again.

And then make your own "Some Surprises Aren't Really Surprises" list. You might even call that a "budget."

YOU WOULDN'T BUY AN $1,800 T-SHIRT

My mom once bought a vacuum cleaner from a door-to-door salesman.

I can't remember if he closed the sale by sucking up a bowling ball or cleaning blood off our carpet or some other feat, but whatever he did, it worked. She went for it. She bought it right there on the spot, much to the chagrin of my father.

Some people don't like door-to-door salesmen. I don't have a problem with them, because I know how hard they actually work and that lots of them are honest, reputable folks. But some people find that method of selling intrusive. It feels a little like they're invading your personal space and convincing you to buy something you really don't want or need. Asking them to leave feels like a mini-confrontation, and that's hard sometimes. But compared to the technique I hate the most, door-to-door salesmen are the kindest people on the planet.

What technique am I so opposed to?

Credit card location marketing.

I invented that term, because I don't know if we as a culture have agreed on one phrase to describe when credit cards go to college campuses, malls, downtown areas and bars to market their wares.

We've been so accustomed to this practice that we don't even notice it, but there are three distinct reasons why this practice should frustrate you:

1 | You should never pay interest on M&M's®.

One Christmas season at the mall, I saw a table offering a free large bag of M&M's if you signed up for a credit card. They were offering a $2 bag of candy as an incentive to pay potentially hundreds, if not thousands of dollars in interest on the purchases you make with that card. Are we Hansel and Gretel, so easily tricked by the promise of "free" candy that we would let the big bad wolf of credit cards into our finances? (Double fairy tale reference? Yahtzee®!)

2 | Credit card companies chum the waters.
When you want to catch a shark, you go to where the sharks feed. You take your boat to seal island and throw your hook in, hoping that in the frenzy of eating, the sharks won't be able to tell the difference between a seal and bait. Credit card companies do the same thing. The reason they go to the mall is that you're already in shopping mode. There's blood in the water; you're already in the mood to spend some money. *Sign up for a credit card I don't need? Sure! The more, the merrier!* Worst of all is credit cards that go on spring break to chase college kids. Convincing beach-crazed college students to sign up for a credit card so they can get a free t-shirt is practically criminal. If any other company preyed on college students

that way, we'd be outraged; but it's normal in the world of credit cards, so we don't even notice. Shame on us.

3 | The only moment they talk about is right now.

The next time you try to buy a used car, I can promise you the dealer will not say, "This car will drive awesome today. It is such a great car for you to drive today. You will love today's performance. Let's not discuss tomorrow, though—I'm not sure it will still be working." That would be ridiculous. We know the car will work right now, but what about later? When it comes to car shopping, we care about the long-term performance of the car. We question the reliability and the maintenance and a million other factors that impact the lifetime of the car. But not when we sign up for a new credit card on location. "Do you want to save 10% on your purchases today?" It's all about the moment. Not tomorrow's purchases, or the long-term interest we'll pay over time. We're told to focus on the purchases that are right in front of us. Carpe diem, seize the credit!

I hope the next time you're approached by a credit card when you are out and about, you'll remember this list. Whether you're a college student in Cancun or a mom at the mall, the principles are the same.

That glittery thing dangling in front of you is actually a fishing hook, not a free t-shirt or a bag of candy.

YOU CAN'T WALK OUT OF TARGET WITH ONLY ONE ITEM

Try it—I dare you. You always go in thinking about that one thing you need. This time will be different, you tell yourself. This time you have a budget. This time there is a debt snowball you're feeding. This time you've got willpower and desire and wait a second, they've got a grocery store in here, too?

When did that happen? Wait one second, this changes everything. I'm not overspending my budget at Target, I'm killing two birds with one stone. I'm home shopping *and* grocery shopping! Think of all the time I'll save. I don't need to be ashamed of this—I should probably call up Dave himself and let him know about all the values.

To not buy this while I am here would be wasteful. Think about the gas savings alone of turning my quick Target trip into a grocery run, too. I am like a grocery gazelle. Take that, debt!

And so it begins. You walk out with a cart instead of a basket. Have you ever had to do the "walk of shame," where in the middle of your shopping trip, you realize your handheld basket is overflowing with purchases and you have to return to the front of the store to get a cart instead? Oh, the embarrassment.

It has little to do with Target, either. That's a great store that I love to shop at. Your "Target" could be Barnes & Noble®, or Best Buy®, or a million other stores. Maybe you casually flirt with the Apple® Store every time you go in the mall. You play with the products, talk yourself into something new, and before you know it, you've made a purchase. You don't even realize it, because you never have to go to the actual counter. You just happen to have a casual conversation with a hip guy named Trey, who just happens to have a mobile cash register in his hand, and he just happens to sell you the computer you've recently always wanted.

Wait, what just happened?

You just fell for your kryptonite store. Like Superman being rendered powerless by the green glowing rock, you are helpless if you get anywhere near it.

The store isn't the enemy. I hope you save up and get the biggest Mac you can fit on your desk. But be honest about the stores you can't handle. Don't make the basket walk of shame. Hit the stores with a game plan, a written list telling you exactly what you're there for—and nothing else. And if you can't fit your purchases in the car you drove to the store, chances are you blew it.

HAVING YOUR WIFE CUT YOUR HAIR iS CHEAP,

THE EVENTUAL **MARRIAGE COUNSELING** IS NOT.

BEWARE THE TEMPTATION
TO DO IT YOURSELF

When you start really hustling on your money, when you start really beating down your debt like a piñata full of delicious candies, you might enter what we call a "savings frenzy." (Okay, we don't call it that. I call it that. That's not an official Dave Ramsey organization term.)

In a savings frenzy, you start to expect every item you buy or every service you purchase to be deeply discounted. And that's a good thing. Now that you're paying in cash, you do have some leverage with the prices you pay. But be careful you don't go overboard with your savings and end up cutting corners by trying to do everything yourself. With internet resources and a thriving Do It Yourself (DIY) culture, it's tempting to try a homemade version of things that are best left to the experts.

In fact, here are three things we recommend you pay for:

1 | Orthodontics

Your daughter needs braces and although you have the money for them, you'd like to see if you could pay next to nothing on the entire package. There's a guy you know who knows a guy who knows a guy who does "mobile braces." He shows up in an Astrovan and will give you braces right in the convenience of your own driveway. And all you have to do is install them yourself and... no. Never DIY your kid's mouth. Don't.

2 | Varmint removal

I once had squirrels in my attic. I tried to save money by catching them myself. How hard could it be? It's a couple of squirrels—they're adorable. They're practically Disney characters. Then my friend Jeff put his leg through our bedroom ceiling when we were chasing them in the attic. And I didn't save money. I had to pay to have the ceiling professionally repaired because there was a gaping hole in it. When it comes to removing critters from your house, don't try to cut corners and handle things yourself. A squirrel is just a rat with a fancy tail, and rats are inconceivably tricky.

3 | Haircuts

I get my hair cut at a national chain place, which is already pretty cheap. But I could go even cheaper and have my wife cut it for me. It's not a bad option, but then I'd have to pay for marriage counseling. I'd have to buy books like *Boundaries* and *The Five Love Languages*, because we'd constantly be yelling at each other. Stick with professionals unless you're bald. If you've got no hair, then enjoy a number one on your head and some cash in your pocket. Win!

Maybe I'm wrong—maybe I could save some money by doing all of those things by myself. Maybe you read this list and thought, *You silly, silly man.* But if I ever find a rattlesnake in my house, I can promise you that I'm calling a professional exterminator. I'm not saving money on pit vipers.

That's where I draw the line, financially speaking: pit vipers.

EXPENSES THAT HAPPEN IN VEGAS DON'T STAY IN VEGAS

Spending money while on vacation doesn't count. I run through hotels like I'm Diddy throwing cash out. Or Dean Martin, depending on what decade you were born in. Either way, I spend money on vacation as if it's not "real money."

It's vacation money. It should even look different than real money. It should be pink and purple and other pastel colors. I'm on vacation! I deserve it! We're going to live forever!

Three weeks later, credit card companies have the audacity—*the audacity!*—to send me bills for my epic jaunt to some distant foreign locale. Like Orlando.

You can't go to Disney World® and save money. You're a princess or a prince. You've dreamt about this your whole life, and this is the moment it all comes together. It's time to shine, or sparkle with

EVERYONE IS A
MILLIONAIRE
ON VACATION.

pixie dust, or whatever it is that means "bright and expensive" at Disney World.

$10 dessert? Yes!

$28 t-shirt? Yes!

$17 light-up plastic thing? I don't even completely know what that is, but yes!

But apparently, bills that happen in Vegas don't stay in Vegas. In fact, they're often like a reverse souvenir. Instead of delighting you when you return, they arrive like a stomach punch in your mailbox after you're back in normal life and have forgotten all about a world where paying $9 for two AA batteries seems perfectly reasonable.

I love Disney World and have been four times in the last two years. But you still shouldn't cheat on your budget when you go on vacation. Plan it. Save for it. And enjoy it! Live it up with the money you've set aside for vacation, but don't pretend for a second that vacation bills don't count. Like Dave says, the best vacation you could ever take is the one that doesn't follow you home.

A PICTURE IS WORTH

A THOUSAND BUCKS.

LET'S GET VISUAL, VISUAL

Did I just make an Olivia Newton John joke about her song "Physical"? Wow, I am so relevant! But don't let the '80s joke distract you from some deep wisdom that—and I hate to exaggerate—will probably change your entire life. Forever. And your kids' lives. And probably your grandkids' lives.

When you start beating your debt, when you lean into it with all you've got, you have to find creative ways to stay motivated. It's a marathon, not a sprint, and you need pick-me-ups to keep going strong. One of my favorites is pretty simple: I make things visual.

Let's face it. I'm a free spirit. I'm an emotional, easily-distracted-by-shiny-objects, creative writer. It's hard for me to get excited about math or numbers or details, so when it came time to pay off some debt, my wife and I created some easy ways to paint a visual picture of what we were doing.

For instance, we didn't just talk about paying off the loan amount on our Toyota® 4-Runner. We drew a 4-Runner on a whiteboard in our laundry room. Every time we paid off a chunk of money, we'd color in part of the 4-Runner on the board. We'd joke around while driving it and say things like, "We own the front seats now! We're working our way to the back."

Having a picture of what we were doing helped us visualize the finish line. It wasn't just some abstract ending point; it was a completely colored-in 4-Runner that we saw every time we did laundry. It gave us an "Eye of the Tiger"–type motivation that helped us push through some of the hard parts of the whole experience.

So if you want to get going and really stay on top of your game, think about ways you can make your hopes and dreams visual. Or as Olivia Newton John reminded us in the '80s, "Let's get visual!"

YOU WILL BREAK UP IN EUROPE

Crazy things happen to us when we fall in like. I didn't say "love"; I most definitely said "like," as that's what usually strikes first when we start dating someone. Like is fun and bright and shiny and fireworks, and then we help pay to have their kitchen remodeled.

Wait, what? What just happened? We're not like that. We wouldn't impulsively remodel our own kitchen for no reason. We'd never ask a near stranger, who is admittedly fun to sit next to in movies, to pay for something so massive. So why are we writing checks to contractors and picking out tile?

We're in like. And like is a pretty powerful thing. But before you jump in with both your heart and your wallet, please be aware of a few things:

IF YOU AND YOUR **BOYFRIEND** **BUY A**  DOG TOGETHER, DO YOU GET **VISITATION RIGHTS** IF YOU BREAK UP **?**

1 | **Paying for someone else's vacation is a great way to ruin a vacation.**

Did he really just buy a mouth-blown pink-and-blue glass dolphin? But he didn't have the money to buy a plane ticket? I had to cover that, but he's dropping money like an '80s rap star. Are you serious? Worst vacation ever. I'm totally dumping this guy in Paris, the city of like.

2 | **Co-signing on a car is something you should abstain from in a relationship.**

Yes, we've been dating for a few months, but what happens if we break up? Every relationship only has two options: marriage or break-up. Do I really feel like we're headed to the altar eventually? Me, her and this brand-new Honda® Accord with a moon roof? This feels iffy. If we break up, do I get visitation rights?

3 | Surgery is a mighty serious way
to spend a date.

Am I a heartless person if I don't contribute
to my boyfriend's surgery? Is my love really
that shallow? I mean after all, if he wants to
have calf implants—if he feels like that's the
missing piece to his life—who am I to deny
him elective leg surgery? Is that the financial
investment I really want to make, though?
Does Dave Ramsey have a chapter about
paying for cosmetic leg surgery?

4 | Buying an expensive animal together is
like purchasing furry dynamite.

I don't even really like dogs, but she does and
I like her, so by extension, I have to have a
pappillon right this second. I can't even say
the name of that breed out loud without
giggling a little. Can you name a dog that
weighs less than a large Snickers® "Rex," or
do you have to automatically name him "Sir
Worthington Mittens?" Probably. And does

this thing really need to eat lamb with capers? I think that dog might be eating better than me. This could be trouble down the road, but I really like her.

Think I'm exaggerating? Ask my friend about the joy of sitting next to her suddenly ex-boyfriend for eight hours on the return flight from the European vacation she paid for. Ask my friends who have a joint-custody arrangement for a golden retriever right now. Ask the thousands of ex-girlfriends who get calls from bill collectors looking for the payments an ex-boyfriend stopped making on a car.

Fall in love. Fall deeply and truly in love. We couldn't be bigger fans of true love.

But be careful about like. Like is expensive.

THE DAVE RAMSEY CORPORATE CREDIT CARD

IS AN ENVELOPE FILLED WITH CASH.

DOES DAVE REALLY BELIEVE THIS STUFF?

When I moved to Nashville, I went to a school event with my wife. While I was there, someone pulled me aside and asked me a whispered question. Here's what he said:

"Tell me the truth—did Dave Ramsey really go bankrupt?"

I wasn't expecting that question. Dave is totally honest about the low point in his life that served as a catalyst for things to come. It's a big, raw part of his story and a key part of why he cares so much about giving hope to other people. He's been at the bottom. He's been harassed by credit card collectors. One even asked his wife, "How could you stay married to someone like that?" Dave's seen the worst.

And it's all true. He lived every bit of it. It's real.

But maybe reading this book, maybe hearing the radio show or even going to one of the events, you've had your doubts. You're curious—does Dave really believe this stuff?

I think that's a good question, and I can't think of a better way to finish this book than by answering it.

Here are four things I've learned about the Dave Ramsey organization now that I work here:

1 | The Dave Ramsey corporate credit card is an envelope filled with cash.

Within my first month of working with Dave, I had to go on a road trip. At most companies, that means you'll get a corporate credit card. Not with Dave Ramsey. Someone handed me an envelope of cash. No card. Just cash. I'm not used to having that much cash on me, and subsequently, I carried it around like a spy with a briefcase handcuffed to him.

2 | **We take credit cards at our live events.**
And cut them up.

Every week, we miss out on thousands of dollars of potential revenue. Why? Because we don't accept credit cards. People ask all the time and feel a little sheepish when we politely refuse, but we just don't take credit cards. Not at our live events, not on our website, not over the phone. Not from individuals or businesses or even churches. We've got to walk the talk.

3 | **Dave Ramsey's wife loves the library.**

Dave always talks about millionaires who drive pretty average vehicles. Not because they have to. Not because they're trying to be a financial martyr. Nope, they do it because they want to, they like to, and they're wired that way. Same with Sharon Ramsey, Dave's wife. The first time I met her, we talked about our mutual love of the library. She goes as often as I do. She can't get enough of the library. Does she need to? No. Does she have to? No. She wants to. She loves books, but she knows that some books are worth reading but maybe not worth buying. She's smart with her money regardless of how much she has.

4 | There are credit-card-sniffing robots.

Okay, we don't have those. Yet. But sometimes people think we do. My friend, a pastor, once came to speak at our weekly devotional meeting. He confessed to me that before he came inside, he took all of his credit cards out of his wallet and hid them in his car. He was afraid that Dave might ask to see his wallet when they first met. Dave didn't, and we don't do any kind of random wallet checks when guests and team members enter the building. But don't think we won't develop those robots. Those are on the way.

I could write a much longer list than that, but the bottom line is that Dave Ramsey lives what he says. And I'm glad he does.

Because although I never thought I'd say this, I think beating debt is fun. I've had a lot of laughs along the way, and I expect a lot more. From baby-proofing your house from 27-year-olds to being financially smarter than cats, this whole thing has been a blast.

And we're not done. Our family is still in the trenches. We're working the plan. We're changing the way we handle money. We're teaching our kids what we wish we knew earlier. If you are, too, if you're right where we are, I hope this book provided a laugh or an I'm-not-the-only-one moment in the middle of your journey toward Financial Peace. We all need that. We all need a boost of encouragement from time to time. We need a push in the right direction.

So get going. Keep laughing. Don't quit.

And long live the gazelles, Baby Steps and the 37 other things you might learn from Dave Ramsey about beating debt!